Praise for *How to Learn a New Language with a Used Brain*

"Lynn McBride's program gives a plethora of practical and yet creative methods for learning languages that readers can use to build their own path, at any age. I wish I had read it before I went to Paris for a month, and I'm glad I have it now for my upcoming trip to Italy and other countries."

–Karen A. Chase (www.karenachase.com), author of *Bonjour 40: A Paris Travel Log*

"I am preparing to spend some time in Italy, and I have some basic conversational skills in Spanish. My plan was to enroll in an online Italian learning program. After reading Lynn's book, I'm taking a totally different approach. Furthermore, I can see here I've made mistakes in becoming fluent in Spanish, and I now know what to do to rectify them. Watch out Italy, here I come...and with confidence! Thank you so much, Lynn!"

–Cynthia Bogart, editor of The Daily Basics (http://thedailybasics.com)

How To

Learn A New Language

With A Used Brain

by Lynn McBride

Published by: Marshall & Gilbert, Victoria, Australia

How to Learn a New Language with a Used Brain

First Marshall & Gilbert Edition 2013

Cover design by Damonza.com

Author Website, www.southernfriedfrench.com

ISBN-13: 978-0-9874548-9-8

For Ron

Table of Contents

"To have another language is to possess a second soul."
Charlemagne

Introduction

My husband and I moved to France from the States as an (early) retirement adventure in 2003, with only the most basic of French language skills. I wish I had a euro for every helpful American friend who offered this breezy assessment before our departure: "Oh, you'll soak up the language in no time!" If only learning a language were so simple.

Ten years later, we speak French imperfectly but comfortably, and we know there's a lot more to language learning than passively "soaking it up". Learning a foreign language requires dedicated effort, and unless you learned it when you were very young, it may be a lifetime endeavor toward a full fluency you may never quite achieve.

Yet I'm hard pressed to come up with a project that is more rewarding. A new language gives you a complete new medium of expression, and opens up a window into a country's culture that you never could have imagined. It also exercises and flexes those used brain muscles, to keep them sharp. Then there is the pleasure of experiencing the new language itself: the rhythm, the melody, the word origins, the cultural quirks.

This book is not about learning a PARTICULAR language, it's a guide to learning ANY language as an adult. If you make a commitment to follow the core program detailed for you in Chapter 3, **Six steps to a Bilingual Life: A Roadmap for the Adult Learner**, a new world will open up to you.

As a former educator and language lover I've worked hard to learn a foreign language and improve the process of doing so, while surrounded by others trying to do the same. In this book are the things I wish I'd known when I started learning a language, solutions that will help you to get on the fast track to speaking and understanding. These are tips that have worked well for me, for many of my expat friends, and for the readers of my blog at Southern Fried French (www.southernfriedfrench.com).

The goal of this book is to arm you with a comprehensive structure for your language study. Most importantly, the program outlined here is not cut and dried, but instead is designed to help you tailor a learning program that works for YOU, one that addresses your style of learning. And you don't need to live in the country of origin to learn your new language, you can go global right at home.

Throughout the book, I've added tips, ideas, and resources collected from our expat friends here in France, from language professionals, and from the faithful readers of my blog, who are voyageurs and learners all. Then in Chapter 4, I've asked several more of these fellow students and professors to offer their best tips and secrets, up close and personal. You won't want to miss this useful and often amusing advice from the front line. From these tips you can pick and choose the resources and ideas that resonate with you, to round out your own personal learning program.

Chapter 5 is a resource guide, a review of the various packaged programs, apps, books, and courses available for language learning. There's also a chapter just for full or part-time expats who want to optimize their learning experience.

I'm happy to have you join us in this journey, no matter what language you're learning or at what level. Now as we say in France: *Allons-y*...off we go!

A special note to readers: because French is my second language, I often use it for examples in this text. But the learning program in this book is a general program applicable to learning ANY foreign language.

ABOUT SOUTHERN FRIED FRENCH

When we moved to France, my husband and I fell serendipitously into an apartment in a medieval château in southern Burgundy, where we lived with the owners, Nicole and Pierre Balvay. I began a blog about our life there, called Southern Fried French (www.southernfriedfrench.com). I blog weekly about French culture, language, cooking, and life in the château. I hope you'll pop right over to the site for a visit, subscribe to the weekly posts, and become a member of the community.

MEET OUR CONTRIBUTORS

In France I've been accompanied on my language learning journey by a large pack of European expats, all multi-lingual or trying to be. Over the years I've picked up many ideas about learning a second language from them, from language teachers, and from those readers of my blog who are learning or teaching languages themselves. Many of them have graciously offered suggestions from their experience.

Among them are experts like Joe Daggett, who has taught languages to international students at the University of South Carolina as well as in Poland, Prague, and Chile. And Dr. Michael Armstrong, who has taught French at Florida Atlantic University for many years. You'll hear from Nicole Balvay of the Château de Balleure (www.lessaveursduchateau), who is a star of my blog at Southern Fried French. Nicole has been teaching French and English for most of her long career as an educator. You'll hear from others who have been doing just what you'll be doing, making language learning a part of daily life. I am grateful to all of them for sharing their wisdom, for allowing me to draw on their experience, and for bringing this book to life.

"If you talk to a man in a language he understands, that goes to his head. If you talk to him in his own language, that goes to his heart."
Nelson Mandela

Chapter 1

The Why and How of Language Learning

I want to share with you a favorite joke, which I heard as soon as we moved abroad. It's attributed to Claude Gagnière, a French writer.

What do you call a person who speaks three languages? Trilingual.

What do you call a person who speaks two languages? Bilingual.

What do you call a person who speaks one language? An American.

Ouch!

And by the way, many other Anglo countries are not far behind us–you know who you are. It's just too easy to skip a foreign language, when one is accustomed to encountering English in so many places around the world. We Anglophones need to catch up with the rest of the world on this score. It's a subject I've come to feel passionate about.

But imagine you are a native speaker of one of the other 7000 languages of the world, or even one of the 12 major ones: meeting a foreigner who speaks, or even tries to speak your language, might not be a common occurrence. Foreigners are often doubly shocked when Americans speak their language; as the joke suggests, we are not known abroad for our mastery of languages other than English. And if you've traveled to a foreign country, or even spoken to a foreigner, you know that the ultimate compliment is to speak their language.

Kicking your cultural acumen up a notch is reason enough to learn a foreign language. It's also an enjoyable challenge, and there are lots of other reasons to tackle a foreign tongue.

Learning a language can be quite a social endeavor, if you choose to make it so. We've enjoyed learning French with our fellow expats here in southern Burgundy. Language learning could be a family project, or a way to make connections online. It's really opened my eyes to meet Europeans here who speak multiple languages effortlessly, giving them a broader global perspective and opportunities for interaction.

There's another important reason to learn a new language. In his article for the *New York Times*, "Why Bilinguals are Smarter", Yudhijit Bhattacharjee writes that "...in recent years, scientists have begun to show that the advantages of bilingualism are even more fundamental than being able to converse with a wider range of people. Being bilingual, it turns out, makes you smarter. It can have a profound effect on your brain, improving cognitive skills not related to language and even shielding against dementia in old age." It's mighty hard to find another avocation that offers such benefits.

Need one more reason to learn a new language? Lera Boroditsky, professor of psychology at Stanford University, writes for the *Wall Street Journal* that language shapes how we see the world, including space, time, and causality. "It turns out," says Boroditsky, "that if you change how people talk, that changes how they think. If people learn another language, they inadvertently also learn a new way of looking at the world. When bilingual people switch from one language to another, they start thinking differently.

"All this new research shows us that the languages we speak not only reflect or express our thoughts, but also shape the very thoughts we wish to express. The structures that exist in our languages profoundly shape how we construct reality, and help make us as smart and sophisticated as we are."

Now let's see: learning a new language is going to keep our minds sharp, make us smarter, turn us into more sophisticated world travelers, show us a new way of seeing and thinking, and maybe even expand our social circle. Sounds pretty good, doesn't it?

Let's begin.

Letting Go of Systematic Learning

I have a friend who is a serious language student. She has purchased every French learning program, CD, DVD, and textbook known to man. She is frustrated by every attempt, and abandons each program in its early stages. "I want to learn French *systematically*," wails this very orderly, organized person. "Why can't I find a program that will do that for me?"

So before we jump into the details of our learning program, it's important to understand the answer to the question above: you *won't* find it. The skills of learning a language are multi-faceted and complicated, and learning to speak is apt to be a messy, disorganized business, with peaks and valleys, hills and plateaus. Yes, you should first systematically work your way through the basic grammar and vocabulary, with a good textbook or program. Then it's time to seriously attack speaking and comprehension. At this stage it may sometimes feel like two steps forward, one back, and you'll be walking a crazy, crooked line. Even when you speak reasonably well, you may find that you can understand one person perfectly, and another not at all. You may be in situations where you comprehend everything, and others where you are lost. This is normal!

Professor Joe Daggett puts it this way: "You can get an insight into the process when you realize that learning a second language proceeds the same way as learning your first language...only you're older so it's not as easy or natural. Damned difficult in fact." And if you've observed children learning a language, you know that complete sentences do not pop out of their mouths first thing.

Even though you can't learn to speak a language in a systematic fashion, that doesn't mean you shouldn't impose some order and discipline on the learning process. We've got some tools in the following chapters to help you proceed step by step, to organize and maximize your studies.

To successfully learn this immensely complex set of skills we call a language, you'll do well to attack it on many fronts simultaneously: speaking, listening, writing, reading, studying, and just absorbing. It's best to set your expectations accordingly, and relax and enjoy what may be, for those of us who are not linguistic mavens, a lifelong project. But that's also the good news! Learning a second language can be fun and sociable. It will constantly challenge and sharpen your mind, not to mention expand your cultural horizons. View the learning journey itself as a fun experience. Your progress, and the worlds that it opens up to you, may amaze you.

Here is my very best advice about learning to speak a second language the EASY way: learn it before you're six years old. You'll absorb it with minimal effort, and no matter what your second language is, it's likely that the rest of your life you'll excel at *all* languages. It will literally re-form your little brain. (Attention parents and grandparents! Early immersion in a second language is the best gift you can give your child. I watch my young grandchildren, who have not lived in

France but attend a French school, move between the two languages effortlessly, their French accent and grammar already exceeding mine.)

If you happen to be over six, you've got a challenge on your hands. Still, whether you're six or 60, the research is mounting that learning a language is the best way to keep your mind fit and supple and to fend off that dreaded dementia. Think of it as an exercise work-out for your brain. Relax, make it FUN while you're at it, and it will serve you well.

The First Step of Your Journey

Now about that used brain: maybe you made a grade you'd rather forget in your high school or college language class. If so, pay it no mind. Unless you're learning a language for business purposes, no one's giving grades now, and you can learn for the pure pleasure of it, the mental challenge, and the rewards of peeking inside the heart and soul of another country and culture.

I believe there are TWO KEYS to learning a language. First, you must make a COMMITMENT to devote some time to it regularly, even if it's just a bit of time every day. The second key is to IMMERSE yourself in it as much as you can. No timid dipping of toes in the water, you've got to dive right into that pool and start swimming. Immersion is the way a child learns to speak, and though we will supplement immersion with grammar and vocabulary study, it remains the best method for learning to truly communicate.

But please don't think you've got to hop on a plane to take that plunge. This book is full of ideas on finding opportunities to LISTEN TO, SPEAK, and UNDERSTAND a language, whether you're learning from your casa in Spain, your Paris flat, or your armchair in Kansas. Greatly aided by modern technology, immersion is possible anywhere and anytime. There are plenty of ideas for you here, and you have only to embrace the ones that fit your learning style.

In the next chapter, we'll be determining your starting level, then looking at an overview of the basic program, **Six Steps to a Bilingual Life: A Roadmap for the Adult Learner.**

"Never make fun of someone who speaks broken English. It means they know another language."
H. Jackson Brown, Jr.

Chapter 2

Two Paths: Outright Beginners, and the Rest of Us

To begin, let's take a look at your level. For the purposes of this learning program, there will be only two camps: 1) absolute beginners, and 2) those who are at least somewhat familiar with the basics of grammar and vocabulary–even if you learned those basics in school and have now forgotten most of them.

1) If You're a Language Virgin:

Congratulations, you're *un débutant* (if French is your new language, that is–love that grand title for a beginner!). If you know none of your chosen language at all, you've got some ground work to do. You must first learn the basics of the language, and this early phase of the program will indeed start out in a systematic fashion. We're not talking mastery here, just familiarity.

You'll need to get up to speed with the fundamentals of grammar and vocabulary, from a textbook or perhaps from a formal class of some kind, whether it's at a school, a university, from a private tutor, an online course, or a packaged program. With the wonderful interactive language programs online now, including full university courses, learning the basics with the help of the internet is a great option, if that's your pleasure. If you like the social interaction of a group or the discipline that a live class or a tutor offers, that may be a better route for you. If you need help choosing a basic grammar program, there are plenty of ideas for you in Chapter 5.

It will help to learn some basic pronunciation, too. However you choose to study, learn from a native speaker if at all possible. It's very important at this stage. If not, try to find someone who is truly fluent and has a wonderful accent, because you're going to be forming your accent and habits early on. They will be hard to break later.

There's no magic to learning the basics—you can do it, it just takes some dedicated study. Short on time to fit it in? Try it in small bites, like a short lesson after lunch, during breakfast, or before bed, but do it every day. You're not looking for perfection or mastery at this point, just an overview of your language and some fundamental abilities.

Start by reading over my basic program, **Six Steps to a Bilingual Life,** summarized at the end of this chapter, and detailed in Chapter 3. In the first section, "Back to the Basics", you'll find more ideas on how to pick up the fundamentals of your new language as a base for further study.

2) If You've Learned or Studied the Basics of your New Language at Some Point:

Most folks who are interested in learning a language have, at some point in their lives, had a class or two in high school or college. There was a time in your past when you learned the basics of grammar and vocabulary, but these may have mostly slipped away from you. You are ready to start the core program.

The Core Program, **Six Steps to a Bilingual Life: A Roadmap for the Adult Learner**

1. BACK, BRIEFLY, TO THE BASICS

...of grammar and vocabulary. Not necessarily to master them, just to review them. You'll be revisiting them as you go along, in many mediums.

2. LISTEN UP

A pesky little problem with talking to someone in your new language: yikes, they talk back! So we'll learn how to ease into talking by first practicing passive listening for comprehension.

3. LEAP TALK PRAY

Jump right in and start talking! Why you must, how to start, whom to talk with, and where to find them.

4. READ LIKE A NATIVE

Read the *right* way, and love it! And write, too.

5. DON'T QUIT NOW

You're in this for the long term. How to keep it fresh and stay motivated.

6. MAKE IT FUN!

Sure it's work, but that doesn't mean it has to be boring.

In the next chapter we'll cover each of these steps in detail. Ready to start? First, go shopping.

Remember when you were young and it was time to go back to school after summer was over? You gathered bundles of freshly sharpened pencils, new crayons, highlighters, pristine notebooks, maybe a new backpack. You were armed and ready to take on the world.

So be young at heart: get yourself a fresh notebook for jotting down questions. Take note of the ideas for learning that you want to work into your personalized program, as you read this book. Then gather your learning materials, and put them into a binder or a basket where you'll have to trip over them daily. If you're of the digital persuasion, grab one of the many task management apps to help you organize your schedule and studies, or a journaling app, or set up your own online system to organize and track your progress (specific tools for this are listed in Chapter 5). Whichever way you choose, your goal is to set up a system to make the **Six Steps to a Bilingual Life** become a part of your routine.

"One language sets you in a corridor for life. Two languages open every door along the way."
Frank Smith

Chapter 3

The Program, Six Steps to a Bilingual Life: A Roadmap for the Adult Learner

To work your way toward fluency, you'll need to address the multiple complex skills needed to learn a language. Each of these skills builds on the other. And with lots of paths to take and skills to master, you'll never be bored!

This chapter contains a multitude of ideas. Pick and choose several ideas from each of the six groups, the ones that work for you, to individualize your program.

I've included **general** suggestions for your program in this chapter. When you've picked the ones you like, you can select **specific** programs in Chapter 5, a review of resources.

And so we start with....

1. BACK, BRIEFLY, TO THE BASICS

You need to be familiar with basic grammar, vocabulary, and pronunciation as a foundation for speaking your new language. If it's been a while, you'll want a quick review. And by a review, I mean just that. Your initial goal does not have to be memorizing every rule. Grammar and vocabulary will be reinforced and addressed in many ways along the path, every time you speak, listen, read, write, or search for a word in the dictionary.

One of my blog readers is Dr. Michael Armstrong, who has taught French at Florida Atlantic University for many years. He explains, "What is most helpful is some basic formal structure, some framework within which to comprehend what you are seeing and hearing each day. It would be helpful to have a fundamental understanding of the unique elements of the new language and why it doesn't work exactly like your maternal language."

There are many ways to do a review of grammar and basic vocabulary. Choose your preferred methods from the following list for some ideas on a multifaceted approach to reviewing the basics of your language. If you're serious about learning a foreign language, and especially if you want to get up to speed quickly, you might select several simultaneous paths.

–Go through a good textbook, for a traditional approach. Consider breaking it down into daily doses. A college bookstore is a great place to browse (in person, or online). Or you might want to pick up a quick, short summary-style review book that is totally manageable, one that you can get through quickly. For his own basic review, our American friend Monty Herron kept such a book by his bed and spent 15 minutes a night studying until he worked his way through it. A set schedule like this makes the process less overwhelming.

You're probably already in possession of a phrasebook in your chosen language, so check out the introductory sections. Many will have basic grammar and pronunciation guides that can get you started.

–Study online. If you want to learn the basics of grammar, verb conjugations, vocabulary, and idioms, there are wonderful resources available now online, in most any format that suits you. The multimedia and interactive aspect of the internet has resulted in some truly creative learning techniques that were not previously possible. Many of these are free.

–Attend a college French class. This is a perfect solution if you're a person who needs a bit of extra structure and discipline. My husband and I both audited a couple of college classes at our local university, right before we moved to France. If your local college doesn't have a formal auditing program (or if you want to bypass it), just phone up the professor–many are happy to let you sit in on an informal basis.

–Sign up for a MOOC. A number of universities, even the most prestigious ones, are now offering Massive Open Online Courses. Some are low cost or even free. This is an exciting new tool for language learning.

–Put a good dictionary on your computer and/or smartphone and tablet, and USE IT every time you need to look up a word or phrase. I have the wonderful Ultralingua dictionary (www.ultralingua.com) on my iPhone, iPad and computer (it's available in multiple languages), so I have no excuse for not looking something up! In addition, there is a verb conjugator and a flash card application.

I find too that browsing the dictionary is a good learning tool. It doesn't sound like it would be, but try it yourself. Pick a common verb or other word that has more than one meaning and start reading. Often you'll see a number of idioms and useful expressions that are great for further study.

Michael Armstrong agrees and has some specifics on how to use a dictionary for study: "Ultralingua has become my 'go-to' app on iPhone and iPad. A year ago I would have recommended that a serious French student get a verb conjugator but I think the Ultralingua programs incorporate most of that utility along with the dictionary function. I would add one thought about dictionary use however, and that is to recommend that your readers go both ways with the dictionary in a two-step process, if there is any doubt about the word." In other words, dictionaries can be your friend, but they're not to be completely trusted! (As my French teacher Nicole is constantly reminding me.) Words have subtle meanings, and if you dig deeper, you may learn nuances of a translation, or even that you've got the wrong word. So if there's any possibility of a double meaning: look up that Italian word, for example; and when you get the English definition, look up THAT word, to get the Italian translation, and see if they are the same.

Michael gives an example: "Our youngest son is taking a college French course now and as part of a project he wanted to describe his own personal character traits. When he looked up the word "character" he found *le personnage*. But this word actually means a fictional character in a play or story. If he had followed up by looking up *personnage* in the French section, he would have realized that he had the wrong word." Doing a cross check will cut down on problems with 'false friends', those treacherous words that sound similar to English but have a slightly (or completely!) different meaning.

Michael offers a second thought on dictionary use, for more advanced students: "At some point in the development of language skills the reader will want (and need) to switch to a dictionary in the target language." I confess I personally haven't switched from a French-English dictionary to a French-French dictionary for my word searches, but it's something I plan to try.

–Look for local language organizations or social groups focused on language practice. The Alliance Française (www.afusa.org), as an example, has chapters in most cities/countries, and they all offer French lessons. There are also websites devoted to bringing folks together with common language interests.

–**Find a Private tutor.** Before we moved to France I found a French woman living in Charleston, and worked weekly with her, hoping to resurrect my old college French. There are also online tutors who will work with you on Skype (www.skype.com) or on Facetime (www.apple.com/ios/facetime). These are low cost or free video phone calls. Friend Barbara McCormick worked with a tutor she found on a visit to the south of France–then continued to work with her on Skype when she got home. Barbara was very pleased with this system.

–**What NOT to do** at this point: attend an immersion program. They're fantastic, but save this until after you've reviewed the basics and can do a little talking. Should you sign up for an immersion program, most of them are going to suggest that you learn, or brush up on, some basic grammar and vocabulary before you arrive.

To develop or boost your conversation skills, it's essential to...

2. LISTEN UP! Practicing Comprehension

When you interact with someone you use speaking and comprehension skills simultaneously. The back-and-forth of conversation is great practice. But actively engaging with an actual human–listening, understanding, and then having to immediately respond to what they're saying–is a big challenge. At first it is likely to strike terror into your heart. Starting with passive listening for comprehension is a good way to ease into your goal of actually conversing.

In this section we'll explore ways to help you practice relaxed, passive listening that does not involve inter-acting with a live person. That's not to say you can't practice conversation in other ways at the same time, if you're comfortable with it. Again, learning your language in a variety of ways is one key to success.

"I'm watching my 15-month-old granddaughter learn to speak," says Joe Daggett. "Right now she's at the stage of listening and comprehending; able only to say a few words. But you can see the process locking in: listening comes first, then speaking."

For comprehension, it's important to listen to your new language in a manner that is appropriate to your level. Otherwise, it's going to be too frustrating. If you're at a beginner to intermediate level, it helps to seek out listening opportunities where you can slow the speaker down, hit the replay button often to re-peat a passage, and/or review the written text of what you're hearing on audio. Repeating, responding at your own pace, and reading out loud will help you, too.

Try these ideas for listening and comprehension prac-tice:

–Listen to language tapes, computer learning programs, videos and podcasts. There are a wealth of choices, which we rate in Chapter 5. Podcasts, which are often free, are super, and you can download them right onto your smart phone or computer.

Online audio language learning programs with videos of native speakers are now available, and they have a couple of really neat and useful tricks up their sleeve. On some of them, the speaker talks at a normal rate, but you can actually slow down the speech to a speed you can understand. Some also have an optional feed at the bottom so you can read what they're saying.

The ability to slow down what you're hearing is a deceptively important one. If the words just fly by, you'll become easily frustrated. But if you can actually slow down the speaker, you'll be surprised at how much you can understand. You can then speed it up gradually.

–If you're mad for movies, this is a perfect avenue for comprehension. They can be difficult to understand, though, depending on the movie. The addition of subtitles (which you can set up on your DVD, for example) is a great trick for helping you get up to speed. Another tip: get ahead of the game by reading as much background info on the film as you can before watching it, to give yourself some context clues.

–Smartphone and tablet apps for learning languages and learning about the culture of your new country are many and varied. Most have visuals or games to make learning more fun.

–Listen to the radio, or watch the news. I like listening to the local news station when I'm in my car in France, because they repeat the news every 15 minutes. If I don't get it the first time around, I have another chance! And with all the internet resources now, it's easy to get foreign stations on your computer as well. Your language skills may need to be at an intermediate level or better, for this exercise to be useful to you.

–Foreign TV shows are great, but choose carefully. Sitcoms in particular are very difficult to understand. Even some fluent speakers here in France have trouble with them. Why? Foreign sitcoms, like American ones, are full of folks who talk rapidly and rely heavily on slang, jokes, and current language. Clear enunciation is not their goal, as it is for a news anchor, for example.

Our British friend Jill, who is quite fluent in French, suggests that "News programs, documentaries and period pieces are a great help. The contemporary police programs are really hard work because of the argot [slang]."

Now you absolutely must...

3. LEAP TALK PRAY: Practicing Speaking and Comprehension

This is often the hardest part of learning a language, especially when you don't live in the country. In many high schools and university classes, this skill has been notoriously short-changed. It is THE most essential practice you'll need. You can study your language exhaustively, but if speaking is your goal and you don't practice it, you're going to be pretty useless when it's Showtime.

Michael Armstrong tells us, "It is important to USE the language. We are often, especially as beginners, so afraid of making a mistake that we don't try to speak often enough. It helps to visualize upcoming situations and practice conversations in one's head." Our friend Chris Wager, who is from the UK but lives in France, sums it up: "You must be unembarrassable!"

To learn to speak, here are RULES NUMBER 1, 2, AND 3: you must TALK! You must do this even when it's uncomfortable, when you're terrified, when everyone's looking at you, when you feel like hiding. If you don't leap right out of your comfort zone, I can almost guarantee that you will never learn to speak. (This is a huge problem with the French, who in general don't speak several languages as other Europeans do. One reason is that many of the French have a horror of making mistakes, so tend not to attempt speaking a foreign language, even if they've studied it.)

In spite of the fear factor in speaking, you'll find that most foreigners, when they realize you're making a valiant effort to speak their language, are happy to be helpful. Martin Worthington says about French, and it applies to any language: "The French are usually amazed (and highly appreciative) if they know that you're a native English speaker trying to kick off the conversation in French, and apart from doing your linguistic development a world of good, it's a great icebreaker too!"

Our egos can get in the way, as Joe Daggett explains: "There are a lot of emotional and personal factors that come into play: inhibition and self-esteem. Many mature people, smart and successful all their lives, just suffer terribly when they have to perform publicly in something they're not very good at, at least initially. They have to suck it up and keep trying."

My best example of where a lack of courage gets you: I once knew of an American woman who had been a high school French teacher for her whole career, and she finally went to Paris for the first time. She was so terrified of making an error that she never spoke a *single* word of French! Now how crazy is that? Imagine the experiences she missed, the opportunity to interact and connect with a culture she'd been teaching about for much of her life.

On the other hand there is the best-selling French author, Mark Levy, who moved to New York, and was fearless. In an interview with Kristin Espinasse of the French-Word-A-Day blog (http://french-word-a-day.typepad.com), he says he often makes embarrassing mistakes. "One example that comes to mind is something I once said to a woman in the street. She was trying to light her cigarette, but her lighter wasn't working, so as a proper French gentleman would, I offered her my own. I asked her, "Do you want my fire?" After she had left, the American friend I was with burst into laughter. When I asked him what was so funny, he explained to me why that had been a ridiculous thing to say. I was absolutely mortified!" Levy adds that he humiliates himself on a daily basis—and by the way he now speaks nearly perfect English.

As an aside, if you want to read an absolutely hilarious account of one language student's embarrassing moments, check out the delightful book *Me Talk Pretty One Day* (http://barclayagency.com/sedaris.html), by humorist David Sedaris. If you're nervous about mistakes, it will make you feel so much better!

Now, when you're ready for that first conversation—how to start? Anne Teichroew of Sidney, British Columbia is a reader of my Southern Fried French blog, and she posed an interesting question: "My question falls in the 'speaking is easier than understanding' category. What on earth do you do in this scenario? You have worked on your accent, formulated your thoughts so when you approach a bona fide French person to ask a question, you feel that there is a remote possibility you will be understood. You take the plunge and ask the question. Then not only are you understood but the French person believes you can actually speak French. They start chatting away to you, believing you understand them. *Quelle horreur!* You have absolutely no idea what they are saying, you feel like a complete idiot and want to run away. *Aidez-moi!* What is the polite thing to say and how can you avert this situation in the first place?"

There's no easy answer, but Joe Daggett has some great suggestions. "I tell my students to disguise what they're doing and think of some pretext to start a low-stress exchange: 'Could you give me directions to _____? Have you eaten at this restaurant? Any good? Nice day, huh? Are you a student? Live around here? Ever been to _____? What's it like? Could you help me with some information for my student project? What do you call that over there?'. That sort of thing."

"So what if they shoot something back at you which you can't understand?" Joe continues. "Well, no need to get uncomfortable. You're allowed to tell them you're just learning the language. 'Could you say that again? A little slower? Using other words?' Okay, now they're on your side, wanting to help. In trying to understand them, listen very closely for key words. Most exchanges like this aren't too abstract and you can, with basic knowledge, get the drift. Repeat those key words (or phrases) to them to see if you understood correctly."

Michael Armstrong adds: "One technique for such situations is to learn REALLY WELL several key phrases, how to pronounce them correctly, and how to riff on those themes (to borrow a guitar concept)." This is one of my favorite approaches as well.

I'll give you an example from my own experience, of the need to practice oral skills and to learn basic phrases. When we moved to France, I had brushed up on my rusty old college French to get ready, but I hadn't SPOKEN much in French. We moved into the château, and we had a very chatty neighbor, the kind who would talk all day if you let her. When we met up I would listen for (quite) a while, then prepare to take my leave. But I was totally unprepared for the phases one uses to exit a conversation. I could say *au revoir* (good-bye) but that was it! In English, I had a wealth of choices: "Gotta go, I'd better run, Well, I'm off, Busy day…" etc. But in French? I just kept repeating *au revoir*, like an idiot, and backing away, and she just kept right on chatting.

Now I know: the French say "*Bon, Allez, Je te laisse, à bientôt alors, à plus tard….*" (Well good, off I go, I have to leave you now, See you soon then, Catch you later…). And yet, I'd never done this very basic role play in a French class. Language teachers, please take note! Phrases people commonly use are what we need to know.

My French teacher here in France, Nicole, zeros in on listening skills for us, and teaches us how the practice of listening to a language can improve our speaking skills as well. "Look carefully at the person who is talking, and mimic them," Nicole says. "That's why it is better to listen to a human being than a recording. It is through listening that you learn new words and expressions, and once you've learned them, use them as often as possible. Whatever you don't use you won't remember for long."

And a reassuring tip from Nicole: "When you listen you needn't try to understand everything. Normally if you understand half of what is said you are OK and you can carry on a conversation."

Some thoughts on perfecting your ACCENT: we'd all love to have a perfect accent but when you learn a language as an adult, mastering an accent is particularly difficult. Joe Daggett suggests that much can be learned by watching and listening. "A lot of it is imitation. You've got to be like little kids, who mimic everything. Make yourself mimic, then try to adjust; get some correction."

There is more to a good accent than pronunciation, however. Joe says, "You start with discrete sounds, then words, then sentences. And it isn't just clear individual sounds, which to us would be roughly represented by letters. There's a *melody* you must work to get: the stress and intonation, the *sound* specific to that language. Think of how differently they strike the ear: a nasally Frenchman, a guttural German, a staccato Spaniard. You've got to put the utterances in that framework."

I couldn't agree more. When I first put my mind not just to speaking correctly but also to speaking more rapidly and conversationally, I found that I needed to tune in to the music and flow of the language, the rise and fall of the entire sentences and phrases as well as the accenting of syllables in individual words. I find the French understand me better as I mimic these patterns.

I take comfort in this fact: when I make my excuses to French friends about my accent, they often say, "Oh but we love an American accent, it's so charming!" My teacher Nicole Balvay agrees. "The goal is not to lose your native accent entirely, but to pronounce words correctly."

It often seems difficult to get the speaking practice you need. Here are some ways:

–Conversation groups. I highly recommend these on one condition: that there is a fluent foreign speaker (hopefully native) leading the group, in which case it's a fabulous way to learn. You get to speak, to listen, to learn from other's mistakes as well as your own, and to ask questions. You'll be in a relaxed environment where it's okay to make errors and you'll have someone there to correct them. It's also great fun. But don't do it with a leaderless group of Anglophones at your level, please, unless that level is very high. It may start out well, but the urge to lapse into English is great. Plus you may just listen to a lot of incorrect chat, without being corrected by someone fluent. I've tried many conversation groups, and I've found them to be a waste of time without a good leader or some native speakers.

I was in a small conversation group in Charleston led by my French friends Mireille and Michel (sponsored by the Alliance Française), and it was a super experience. We chatted about all sorts of things, and the teachers corrected at least the major mistakes. And as we talked, grammar questions that came up could be immediately addressed.

Nicole Balvay of the Château de Balleure leads a weekly conversation group for expats here in France. We are all intermediate to advanced speakers. Our homework assignment is to jot down questions during the week, words or phrases that have tripped us up. When the questions are all answered, we talk about French culture, politics, and so on, over coffee.

It's one of the big social events of the week, and so enjoyable and useful.

These groups are most effective if everyone is at a similar level. But don't be concerned if you're in a group where you are the weakest speaker or you're just a little bit beyond your comfort zone. Even just listening will help you with your comprehension. If the group is far too advanced for you, however, it may just lead to frustration.

–**Language meet-up groups** or international alliance groups for the language you're studying are great places to find someone to converse with. And now online there are a number of interesting language exchange groups which will match you up with a native speaker.

I'll use French here as an example of the benefits of a meet-up group. (There are ideas for other groups in the resource review in Chapter 5.) Francophiles are lucky to have the Alliance Française (www.afusa.org) available in most cities. Their mission is to promote France and the French language. The members are typically both French expats and Francophiles, so you're very likely to find some patient person to practice your French with. Meetings are designed as casual social events, often celebrating French holidays in the traditional style; in Charleston, South Carolina where we lived we had about 50 people at each gathering. The Alliance also offers language lessons with native speakers.

At these meetings, English is the common language, though you hear some French here and there. Early on I met a lovely French woman named Myrtille. My spoken French at this time was awful, but whenever she saw me at the meetings, she would say to me, firmly: "Lynn, *nous allons parler un peu de français ensemble*" (We're going to speak a little French together.) Which would send me into a bit of a panic, but I did it, and was very grateful to her for giving me a little push.

–Try a private tutor. Be sure to tell your tutor your goal: you want to avoid English, and to push yourself to speak. Teachers are prone to lapse into English too, especially if they speak it well.

–Talk to yourself! Or your dog. As you do the dishes or in the shower, have a little conversation with yourself, out loud if possible. If nothing else it will generate questions for your French class, as you come across phrases you need to know. Ignore that withering look from your cat, and carry on.

–Learn your new language in phrases that you can use, instead of just learning verbs and other vocabulary. This is my personal bit of advice, gleaned from experience. Learning common phrases will help you because they follow the rhythm and unique structure of the language. I collect them and hoard them like jewels, hoping that if I learn enough of them, I can pluck them from my mental list as needed and rattle them off like a native.

My questions to Nicole, at our French class, almost always go like this: "How do the French say 'It's not worth the trouble'? How do you say, 'Easy does it'? What's the best way to say 'It happened out of the blue'?" If you use these common phrases properly, instead of just translating them from English, you'll sound much more like a native speaker.

–Go to an immersion program. Before moving to France, we went to the Institut de Français (http://www.institutdefrancais.com) in Villefranche-sur-Mer, for a month. There are many immersion programs in all languages, all over the world. It's a fun (but intense) experience, and you'll get lots of practice. I find, though, that it's best not to get your expectations too high; you'll practice, but you can't learn to speak in just a month. It's also more challenging than you can imagine. Abandoning your native language for eight or more hours a day is tough, so be prepared for hard work. It's really an experience like no other.

There is one particular gift that an immersion program offers, as our friend Bennett Gates, who is in the process of learning French, explains: "If you're trying to move from survival French to conversational French, there's only one word: IMMERSION. No English, ever, for the length of the immersion, preferably two weeks or more. You won't suddenly become fluent (sooner or later, you have to master that grammar) but with a true immersion something quite wonderful happens: *you lose your fear of trying to speak French*. And until that happens, you'll avoid speaking,

35

and unless you speak, you'll never move up from survival to conversational French."

–Create your OWN personal, total (or nearly) **immersion program**. This idea is for the truly hard core among you. With all the new technology available, you can immerse yourself mighty deep into a foreign language, right in your own country.

So here we go. If you're courageous, do all these things simultaneously:

Use the internet, watch TV and listen to the radio only in your target language. The same with reading: no books, magazines, newspapers or blogs in English. Set your computer up in your new language, and your Google searches, maybe even your keyboard. Join an online chat community with native speakers, or hang out with them in person if you can. Do crossword puzzles in your new language. You can even set up your GPS to speak to you in a foreign language. Good luck!

Even if conversing is your only goal, you should…

4. READ LIKE A NATIVE: Reading (and writing) in Your New Language

"Speaking and understanding trump everything in the process for the second-language learner," Joe Daggett tells us. "Listening and speaking are the foundation; reading and writing are subsequent stages."

Why read? It will reinforce your grammar and build your vocabulary. It will help you get used to the different sentence structure of the language. It will make you more comfortable with the language, and it will help you learn common phrases in everyday conversation. If you're primarily a visual learner, you'll find reading particularly helpful.

Writing for the *New York Times* in "My Life's Sentences", Jhumpa Lahiri describes her connection with reading. "Knowing–and learning to read in–a foreign tongue heightens and complicates my relationship to sentences," she says. "For some time now, I have been reading predominantly in Italian. I experience these novels and stories differently. I take no sentence for granted. I am more conscious of them. I work harder to know them. I pause to look something up, I puzzle over syntax I am still assimilating. Each sentence yields a twin, translated version of itself. When the filter of a second language falls away, my connection to these sentences, though more basic, feels purer, at times more intimate, than when I read in English."

Now, WHAT to read? Whatever you enjoy reading in English, read it in your new language. Do you love home and garden magazines? Are you a news junkie? Murder mysteries, chick lit? Biographies? The more fun is it for you, the better the chance you'll stick with it.

If you're at a beginner level, try this trick: read children's books, or young adult books. But you'll need to choose carefully. Pick a traditional story (a tale you're familiar with is a good idea), not one that plays games with words, as children's books often do.

If you read in a foreign language, at a certain level you will eventually encounter this dilemma--everyone does! *Should I just read for pleasure, getting only the gist of it, or should I be diligent and stop and look up every word or phrase I don't know?* The problem you'll face is this: if you just keep reading without the dictionary, you may enjoy it more. If you look up every word, you will learn more, but it may become too much work and you're very likely to abandon reading altogether.

So what's a reader to do? Here are some possible solutions. I use them all.

–Use a highlighter pen (or the highlighter function on your tablet reader) to mark the words and phrases you want to look up. Then you can read, without stopping, for enjoyment, as you would a book in English. Later on, when you're in the mood for a serious language lesson, you can sit down with your dictionary. And if you never get around to it, you've still absorbed something just from reading.

–Try bilingual books. I think they're super, especially when you first begin to read. In these books one side of the page is in a foreign language, and the facing page is the English translation. They're perfect for advanced beginners or intermediate students, and there's no need to look up words or phrases, you just refer to the opposite page.

–Get the gist. Friends here in Burgundy, Chris and Richard Wager, are both fluent in French after lots of study. They recommend reading as one of their favorite learning tools. Here is what Chris has to say: "The method we really found useful to learn French was to read, which I know a lot of people find off-putting. We used electronic translators to look up words and store them in lists and then we tested each other. We forget a lot, of course, but we also remember a few. I think what got us through reading was not to go for the detail, but to get the gist. If you are too conscientious you just get fed up and stop. We also have a very good grammar book which Richard consults, particularly with regard to things like subjunctives, which I like to pretend don't exist. In consequence, his French is better than mine."

A note on choosing books which are translated from the original English: our French teacher, Nicole, cautions that one should read books written in the original language, not translations. The language and sentence structure will be truer. In a perfect world she's right. But I often find that if I read something I have some familiarity with, I'm more inclined to stick with it. If I know the author, I can choose something that's sure to be simple and engaging. Example: the French are mad for British author Agatha Christie, you can pick up a few of her paperbacks at any French *vide grenier* (empty attic sale) or bookstore. I know they're going to be simply written, straightforward and entertaining, so I read them in French. What's important in my mind is to find something that I WILL pick up and read, and not leave languishing on my bedside table. If you're a purist, however, please do search out books written by native speakers which you think will really pique your interest, as Nicole recommends.

Now how about **WRITING** in your new language? This is a skill you should practice, especially if:

1. You enjoy writing.

2. You're a visual learner.

3. You plan on living in a country where your new language is spoken (in which case you're going to need this skill often).

4. You have some other specific use for writing skills.

For many people, good writing in a foreign language is a nice-to-have but not essential skill. It depends entirely on your needs and learning style. If you need it and/or enjoy it, practice it. It's also a wonderful way to learn the language visually. However, for many people who are learning a language for fun or oral use, the fact is that it's going to be the least important, least-used skill.

Do you like to write? Try your hand at poetry or a short story. Simply sitting down with a dictionary and doing a written translation of a passage in a book or magazine that interests you can be a surprisingly useful exercise as well.

My friend Bennett believes writing is crucial. "Writing in French has been, for me, essential. It makes a link between printed and spoken words that really helps your memory, something most older students can appreciate."

You're making progress, now here's how to...

5. KEEP IT GOING

Language fatigue can set in after the initial excitement, and that's when it's time to change strategies. Try a new learning program, book, or medium. Mixing it up is a good thing, and remember, being systematic in your approach is not required or really even possible.

Here's great advice from seasoned teacher Joe Daggett: "Motivation is supremely important. My students all have their eyes on the prize—an American university degree. But many of them dawdle because it's too hard. Experience tells me that the best learners are the most motivated ones, the ones who really, seriously want to do it and realize they can because millions of others, no smarter than they, have succeeded. They can be motivated by pride, the challenge, parental pressure, the promise of economic reward, whatever. But the ones who are willing to work hardest do the best."

These ideas will help you keep your program going:

–Study the culture and the country to keep your interest up. I do this by subscribing to magazines about France, designed for expats, such as *France* and *Living France* (www.completefrance.com). In addition to articles on travel and culture, this genre of magazines typically has language learning features, like bi-lingual articles or quizzes. There are magazines of this type for other countries and languages, of course.

–**Collect phrases** and add them to your daily agenda book or program. Study a phrase, then add it to a page in your calendar a month from now, and see if you remember it. And try to USE the phrase that very day, in conversation or writing. Learn a phrase a day and you'll be surprised at how rapidly you increase your fluency.

–**Make language learning a part of your daily life**. our friends Monty and Ali Herron have a chalkboard in their kitchen where they routinely write phrases or words they're trying to learn. I learn something new from their board every time I visit. I especially admire the discipline of our English friend Richard Wager. He has a favorite French language textbook. Each year, he re-reads it straight through. But he does this in small bits, by reading a lesson each day.

–**Enlist a friend to study and practice with you.** This can be the best motivator of all.

–**Play Word Games** with your smart phone, tablet, or computer. There are tons of apps, puzzles, games, and quizzes to choose from. Play Scrabble for example, or do crossword puzzles.

Here's a game I sometimes play with fellow expats: in conversation we often come up with a new phrase that no one has heard of before--perhaps we encounter it when we're traveling together, or when a waiter uses it at a restaurant. We then propose a contest: who can be the first to spring it on the group later on, by working it into a conversation?

I play a similar game with my husband. One of us comes up with a new word or phrase; then we challenge each other to pop it into the conversation that day. The winner gets...well, that's for you to decide.

–Keep a running list of questions for your teacher. These might be foreign words/phrases that you've heard but don't understand; or perhaps English phrases/idioms that you want to know how to translate. Post the list in a prominent spot in your home and add to it whenever you encounter something difficult.

–Type up or dictate your notes after a class or conversation group. It reinforces what you've learned, and also organizes your notes on the computer where you can revisit them. Consider putting them on your mobile devices as well. A plane ride or a long wait anywhere is a perfect opportunity to do a review. My friend Bennett puts his new words and phrases on flashcards, as a tool for self-testing. Ultralingua (http://www.ultralingua.com) dictionary programs include flash card capabilities, and there are flash card apps for smart phones and tablets available as well.

–Read and subscribe to blogs about the country of the language you're studying--there are so many fun blogs now about travel, culture, language, and expat life. I try to throw French words and phrases into each post at my blog at Southern Fried French, for example, something many expat bloggers do. There are a number of blogs exclusively devoted to language learning, too.

–Step outside of your comfort zone. "Challenge yourself," says Joe Daggett. "Go someplace interesting where you know there's nobody who speaks your language and you're going to be on your own. Nothing bad's going to happen and every situation that you successfully survive using the target language will give your confidence a little boost."

Along the way, why not...

6. MAKE IT FUN!

Keeping it fun and fresh means it's much more likely that you'll stick with the program.

"Always try to have fun; enjoy what you're doing," says teacher Joe Daggett. "Be ready to laugh at your stumbles. Don't beat yourself up emotionally. And be patient; resign yourself to the fact that it will not happen fast."

Consider these ideas, to make learning fun instead of a chore:

–Travel to a country that speaks your new language, if you can. If the main country is far away, you may find enclaves such as territories, cities or island colonies where they speak your second language.

–**Sing!** My Dutch friend Frank speaks several languages. He loves music and is forever bursting into song. "To learn a new language," Frank says, "I like to listen to and sing songs, in particular those that are sung very clearly. I don't know if this is a very practical learning tool, but it works for me alright!"

–**Play.** Think outside of the box to come up with new experiences. Studying Italian? Take cooking classes in Italian. If Spanish is your thing, try cooking with Spanish recipes or cookbooks. Find some music in your new language, and learn the lyrics. (Children's song collections, with their fun and simple lyrics, are great if you're a beginner. Teach them to your kids!) Find a native speaker on Facebook or Twitter to connect with. Surf around to the many wonderful expat sites. Attend language classes with your kids or grandkids. Make some audio tapes of yourself, to work on your accent. Play word games in your new language. My friend Bennett says, "I just noted that my iPad Scrabble app–which is great–allows you to choose French as the language. But it's hard to rack up the big points using two-syllable words like *en* and *ou*!"

–**Learn your new language with a friend**, or family member. Even an online friend will do. Some commercial language packages now offer this option with their programs.

–**Learn your language "on the pillow"!** Are you single and available? They say the very best way to learn French, for example, is to get a French girl-

friend/boyfriend. Obviously this is not a practical solution for everyone and my husband is firmly forbidden from employing this technique.

Now it's time for...

A LITTLE HELP FROM OUR FRIENDS

If you've followed this program, then you've brushed
up on your basics through books, online learning,
formal classes, and maybe some tutoring. You've
tuned in to TV and radio, movies and podcasts to
better your comprehension. You've dared to speak
up, practicing your new language in conversation
groups, with private tutors, and with immersion of all
kinds. You've tried reading for pleasure with bilingual
books, magazines, or even children's books. You've
sharpened up your written French. Along the way,
you've kept it fun and active with play, social connections, travel, word games, and a dip into a new culture.

It's a lot of work, but you're not alone in this language
adventure. It's time to hear from those who are out in
the field, boldly moving forward with their own language programs. They have a thing or two to teach us,
and some ideas you may find surprising.

"Language shapes the way we think, and determines what we can think about."
Benjamin Lee Whorf

Chapter 4

Voices of Experience: Language Learners Share Their Secrets

This chapter is a gold mine. In my description of the **Six Steps to a Bilingual Life**, you've heard from expats and language teachers. Here are more voices, of those who are successfully learning and/or teaching languages, and the methods they've gleaned, borrowed, or discovered that work best for them.

These voices include educators, friends studying languages, and expats who live or have lived in foreign countries; and readers of the Southern Fried French blog, who are a diverse lot of travelers and seekers. Please note: French is used in many of these examples, but just substitute the name of the language you're learning. These methods are universal.

Among our contributors are linguists who speak multiple languages and tell us how they personally accomplished this feat. Others are simply enthusiasts struggling along as best they can. They learn with music, with friends, with games, with disciplined study, or with their own improvised techniques. You'll find their stories helpful, surprising, amusing, and inspiring.

Since everyone learns a bit differently, you're bound to find something here that will strike a chord for you. This is your opportunity to further tailor your language learning program to suit YOUR needs.

And now, language learning secrets from those who are out there in the trenches, students of every age and ability level. Here are their stories.

BE A CLOWN!

From Mark Kane, Des Moines, Iowa, fine art photographer and Chief groundskeeper of Your Garden Show (www.yourgardenshow.com)

"One aid is allowing yourself to feel clownish. You'll learn pronunciation much faster if you let your lips and tongue and vocal cords perform outlandish imitations of a French speaker in spite of how foolish these physical changes will make you feel (sort of like a version of Charles Boyer singing 'sank heaven for leetle girls'). Another way of thinking about this: self-consciousness stunts your progress."

CHAT UP A CUTE POLICEMAN, OR BORROW A FRIEND'S HUSBAND

From Jacki, Boise, Idaho

"You simply have to not be embarrassed to try to speak the language! I have been to France three times now, but never made much progress with the language—I was always tongue-tied. Then, my friend and I rented an apartment in Sanary-sur-Mer a couple of years ago. The guidebooks said it was kind of a tourist town, but it neglected to say FRENCH tourists, not English speaking ones. My language skills really improved while I was there, because there was no choice but to try to speak French—very few people spoke any English at all! You can imagine the comical scene—me trying to convince the local *gendarme* (ooh la la and he was so cute!) not to tow our car away because it was broken and a mechanic was on the way! All in French, *mais oui!*

When it comes to friends, the combo of a wife who speaks good English and a husband who speaks none is ideal. While staying with such a couple in France, I was forced into speaking French with Albert while his wife and daughter were away at work every day. Necessity is the mother of... foreign language improvement!"

LET THE NEIGHBORS LAUGH

From Chris Wager, Tournus, France and Leicester, England

"Richard and I already had a reasonable grounding in grammar when we arrived here so that was a solid base. However, stringing a sentence together was very difficult when we first came to France and we lacked basic vocabulary.

We had two main methods of learning. We got French people to talk and listen to us as much as possible and various wonderful souls were very helpful and put up with us on a regular basis for quite a while.

We still do not get the practice we need and my theory is that you have to have a job or a French partner/spouse/hot date to really learn properly. I don't think that I will ever have to be in that position.

I must say that if I had to learn another language I would learn a whole lot of vocabulary and basic phrases then string together the words as best I could. At least you communicate that way. I would not try to be particularly correct to start with at least. It just slows communication. Last but not least you have to be 'unembarrassable'. Our neighbors quote my howlers around the district. I provide them with great amusement."

KEEP YOUR BRAIN YOUNG

From Deery Walker, Jackson, Mississippi

"As *une femme d'un certain âge* and a diehard Francophile, I have discovered one of my favorite ways to increase my comprehension of *la langue française* and to keep my mind young is to work a French crossword puzzle (*mots croisés*). Actually it's a double dose of medicine since learning a new language and working crossword puzzles are two of the top ways suggested by the experts (who they are, *je ne sais pas*) to enhance brain function. The jury is still out on whether it's working for me, but at least I'm having fun trying."

SECRETS OF A MULTILINGUAL SPEAKER

From Colette, a Canadian living in North Carolina

"French is my mother tongue and I do have a passion for languages, mostly because it opens up our minds to a new culture which cannot be understood without learning its language. I joined the Canadian Foreign Service in 1975 and traveled the world until I retired in 2009 out of Geneva, Switzerland. I studied Russian, Japanese, Arabic, and am now fluent in Spanish and very comfortable in Italian.

The best way for me to learn is immersion. I find a friend who is willing to help and has the patience in the first few months to keep speaking to me in the language I am learning. At first I understand next to nothing but my ear gets used to the rhythm. It is an important phase to learn where the accents are. When I learned Spanish at the UN School of Languages in Geneva, I had classes twice a week for two hours, but I made friends with the daughter of a colleague of mine who was from Colombia. We met every day at lunch, and she called me every night to talk for at least another hour. She never spoke French to me, she stuck to Spanish and promised that after six months I would be on my way. She was right. The first three months were very hard, but I studied the grammar and memorized the vocabulary.

Learning a new language is like learning anything else in life, one must have the will to learn, be interested in the subject with passion. In short, one must enjoy the experience of learning, keeping in mind the great satisfaction it brings at the end, of conversing with someone from another country in his/her language.

I never became fluent in Russian, Japanese or Arabic but spoke it well enough to understand their culture, and I came to the realization that as different as these cultures are from my own, we all have our humanity in common. In the end, all the citizens of the world have the same goals: the search for love, raising a family, and work we enjoy."

IF YOU'RE AN AUDITORY LEARNER...

From Patricia Glee Smith, a fine art painter from Illinois, living in Italy (www.patricia-glee-smith.com)

"When I had to learn German, I listened to tapes while I was painting or doing anything that didn't require too much concentration. I also studied the textbook from time to time, but mainly listened, or didn't listen but used it as a background noise. The language seeped in, so to speak. The first time I went to Germany, phrases came out of my mouth. Of course you can't be in a hurry with this method."

A CLASS CAN BE HELPFUL–OR NOT

From Beth Craig, Miami

"I studied Spanish in Madrid at a class where we studied in a book, did homework, and studied conjugation of verbs. I really applied myself to it three or four hours a day, as I had the time to do so. My Spanish remained poor. I went to Berlitz, and shared a class with a friend. The three of us did conversation only—we would bring in the newspapers or *HOLA* magazine (www.hola.com) and just start speaking. The teacher would get us to use two tenses in the sentences, always pushing us–this was fantastic and I progressed quickly."

USING FILMS AS A TOOL

From Josh Chalmers of the Earth2Company (www.earth2company.com)

"Here's my tip, something I started doing this year and have already found to be my own mini-immersion tool, and helpful–I put movies on that I know well, from my DVD collection, and put subtiling on in FRENCH (not all movies have this feature, of course). Then, I focus on the subtitles more, and watch a familiar movie with French in my brain instead of English. It has been really fun. You can extend that experience to changing the spoken language, if it's available, to French, too, so you watch a dubbed version. Because of the familiarity of the movie I choose, I find myself engaged in the language switch pretty quickly and French words and phrases are starting to feel like old friends. Like *L'attaque Des Tomates Tueuses* (Attack of the Killer Tomatoes), *Le Magicien d'Oz* (The Wizard of Oz,) *L'un A Survolé Le Nid De Coucou* (One Flew over the Cuckoo's Nest)."

INSPIRED, BUT STARTING FROM GROUND ZERO

From Melvin R. Dickerson of Tecumseh, Michigan

"I'm preparing to go meet with my French coach at the café as I try to do each week. And that is one of my MOST important language learning suggestions. There are others including learning to sing some of Celine Dion's great French songs while vigorously peddling a stationary bike.

With my French coach, really it is a chat about anything and everything that either of us wants to talk about, almost all in French. She always starts by asking me what I did last week and I tell her she is just like *une psychiatre*, a psychiatrist, with similar benefits only much less expensive.

I often find especially the evening before sessions with my coach that I begin to create French conversations in my head in anticipation of our meeting. Often that conversation continues most of the way home and even while working in the yard. Seems a bit obsessive to me but it works. I'm thinking in French. Sometimes I go to sleep thinking in French. Actually I may speak much better French in my dreams than in reality!

Thirty-three years after my first round of French classes I went to France. That was in 1999 and I could order some *pain* (bread) and *une pomme* (apple) at the *épicerie* (little grocery store) and not a lot more. I learned one of my favorite French words while eating lunch in a tiny restaurant near Les Jardins du Luxembourg in Paris. *Incroyable*! (unbelievable), exclaimed an elderly French gentleman upon rising to leave after his meal, while intently looking at my friend and me, who had been blabbering in English next to his table. I was quite overjoyed to have been the object of such an intense expression of French disbelief and to learn this great word.

After one week in France I returned home thoroughly hooked on the place and determined to learn to speak French and return to see much more of France for a whole month. This is my advice and what worked for me.

For starters get a good small phrase book like Lonely Planet. Read it and speak the phrases out loud. It doesn't matter what you sound like. There are many essential phrases in the phrase book. Start repeating the words spoken by the French reporter on the tape *out loud* and try to pronounce them using the guide. Your speaking may sound a bit humorous to French speakers but people aren't really laughing at you and anyway you can laugh too. Smiling and laughing is good social grease. Most people will want to help when you get to that point.

Listen to tapes on the commute to work. It really helped me understand spoken French. If there is a text with it, it's helpful to understand all the meanings. I just played them over and over until I could understand all the words all the way through each tape.

In the US I watch TV5 Monde (www.tv5.org) on the television. It's great stuff. People in foreign countries learn their new language mostly from radio and television. I can actually understand many songs now and even some jokes. Those and some movies are the hardest part.

Get a good French/English dictionary. Use it. In a short time it should look pretty dirty around the edges. Read a lot of French at whatever level you can and read it out loud. Read in a loud voice, speak it! For some reason your brain is more impressed by what you say out loud than by what you think. Psychologists have tested the idea and it is so. It even works just to lift your spirits like a walk in the woods.

The exercises above are mostly passive learning and that only goes so far. To speak is different.

In 2010 I arrived at my favorite hotel in Bordeaux and Erik, the *propriétaire* (owner), engaged me in a half hour chat about my trip and our meetings during my past visits before he even thought of checking me in. All in French. Fantastic and I loved it! Except for a few times when French folks wanted to speak English, I spent the whole month speaking only French—imperfectly, but still...loving every minute.

Total immersion is probably the best, most natural, and most efficient way to learn a language. The essential part of that method is that one MUST speak the language a lot every day. Starting to speak a foreign language ASAP is the most essential tool, in my opinion, to learn the language. Learning to speak a language is not a passive sport."

WARNING! CHOOSE YOUR (JAPANESE) TEACHER WELL

From J.D, Virginia

"Years ago while living in Japan, I attempted to learn spoken Japanese. I knew I would be overwhelmed trying to learn to write! After a few months of clandestine lessons with a female member of my office staff, I ventured out to the local market to test my skills. I thought I was doing pretty well regardless of the few snickers and bashful grins by the various women in the store. As I was checking out with the male owner of the grocery store, he casually whispered to me in English, "I think you learned your Japanese from a young lady?" I confirmed his suspicion, but inquired further, 'How would you know that?'

It seems I was using many of the colloquial, hip, and definitely female expressions in my speech which was NOT the expected vocabulary."

NEVER FORGET A PHRASE

From Kiki of Snefnug Studio
(www.snefnugstudio.com), watercolor artist from
Boise, Idaho, living in Vallauris, France

"I live in France, and if one carries around a small notebook (for me one in every purse), then when you ask a French person 'How do you say that in

French?', one can write the answer down—even if it is just a phonetic spelling. That way it sort of sets it in your mind how you say this or that because you had to write it down."

BE BOLD!

From Diane Stanley, Oak Ridge, New Jersey

"1. Never be afraid to speak with anyone who is French. I've started to talk with complete strangers whom I suspect are French-speaking, whether in a line at a bus or at Disney World, at a restaurant, wherever. I live in northern New Jersey, closer to Manhattan, so maybe it is easier to find French speaking people.

2. Spend at least 20-30 minutes each day on your target language, but whatever you do, keep it interesting.

3. Use a good online dictionary for the target language.

4. Join a French speaking club such as the Alliance Française. Or start your own club of even one or two people."

LISTEN, EMULATE, AND DON'T FORGET THE WINE

From Michaela Rodeno, Oakville, Napa Valley, of Villa Ragazzi Wine (www.villaragazziwine.com)

"I have two tips to consider, one simple and one complex.

The complex one first: spend time in a language lab with headphones on, intently listening to and emulating tapes of native speakers. That's how I (even after years of studying French rather successfully) finally understood the minute distinctions in sounds that can make or break you in a conversation—I'm sure we've all experienced the blank stare of a French person who doesn't comprehend the correct word that you have mispronounced ever so slightly.

The easy one relates to relaxing and going with the flow. I actually start understanding Italian pretty well and even start speaking it (rather badly, but Italians are very kind about trying to understand) after several glasses of wine, and my fluent French gets very fluent indeed. Yet another good reason to drink wine. I suppose there are other ways to relax, but this is my favorite."

LINKING ROMANCE LANGUAGES

From Ido Cervantes, Utah, of the Arce French of Heart blog (http://arcefrenchofheart.blogspot.fr)

"One thing I noticed about French is that many words are very similar to Spanish. I speak perfect Spanish so for me it is better to study French, but relating it to the Spanish I know. Also the words in the sentences are in the same order, unlike in English. I keep a notebook with sentences in Spanish and then translate them to French, it kind of works for me that way. If I listen to a word I have to know how to spell it, that way I never forget that word."

DILIGENCE WILL BE REWARDED

From Jill in Burgundy

"I'm afraid my only tip is that you have to put in the hours of study! When I first arrived in France I had one-to-one lessons with my French tutor twice a week for 90 minutes each lesson (at 7:00 am!! So I could get to work by 9:00), and then homework in between. I did that for three or four years."

PACK A FUN READ FOR THE ROAD

From Sue Otto, Los Angeles, California

"Having studied French for two-thirds of my life, I keep my skills current with a subscription to *Paris Match* Magazine (www.parismatch.com). Although it is far from highbrow reading, the current affairs articles, the celeb gossip and the peek into French life keep my vocabulary fresh and up-to-date. I prefer having a copy of the magazine to the online version as I throw the weekly magazine in my bag and take it with me when I eat lunch, stop for coffee, etc."

BET YOU HAVEN'T TRIED THIS ONE!

From Katy George, Taos, New Mexico, formerly of Paris

"Put a list of 10 vocabulary words on a card and tack it up at eye level just facing the toilet (or behind it for guys). That way, every pee is a review of those words. Once you have them all, change to a new list. This really helped me increase my vocabulary. Never took more than two days to master a list.

Another thing that helped with my French pronunciation was exercising my lips several times a day. Stretching, ooohing, eeeing, all to develop my ability to speak more in the front of my mouth, as one must do with French. I did it for six weeks and all my French friends noticed!"

PUTTING LATIN TO GOOD USE

From Sue Wallace, Frederick, Maryland

"If you've taken years of Latin in Catholic School, you probably still own more root words than you realize. This helps me associate/translate. If you like to cook/eat, starting with learning menu/food words gives you a language boost, especially when you can then translate for friends at a restaurant dining table, which is motivational and an ego boost. My husband isn't a word person, he's a pilot. He does so well in a French restaurant that his brother told their Mom, 'Bill is fluent in French'. Actually, I'm still waiting for him to get a grip on English! (He's 69.) *M'aidez!*–help me!"

A LIFETIME PROJECT

From Joan Alderdice of Belfast, Northern Ireland, and Burgundy

"I was thinking about what I could add to the gathering knowledge on learning a foreign language. It is certainly a lifetime's project. I despair when I hear people say 'you must be fluent now'. I feel I'll never be fluent, as the more you know the more there is to learn, but I will keep working at it!

I have been a subscriber for a number of years to a language learning magazine (*La Vie en France*, US; *La Vie Outre-Manche*, UK, www.concordefrench.com). There are great articles, each with a short vocabulary list covering current affairs, tourism, history, politics, sport, regions to visit, and a very helpful grammar section on a particular theme. This is very useful."

VIRTUAL CONNECTIONS

From Georges Cerles, Online French Teacher/Tutor (www.tutorprofiles.com/profile-georges-cerle)

"I teach French online and I am having a great time with students all over the world...Skype and a Smart Board [an interactive whiteboard used by educators] do the trick...it's fun and it works. Working with a native speaker is the key, I think. I studied Spanish and

English with native speakers and always felt they gave me 200% of themselves."

UNIQUE LANGUAGE TOOL: NAUGHTY DRINKING SONGS

From Mary Remmel Wohlleb, Little Rock, Arkansas

"My tip comes from the linguistic premise that melody helps with memory.

My personal anecdotal experience (which made me a believer) is that before I had studied much Spanish, a friend taught me a (naughty) Spanish drinking song. Later, when I took a Spanish class and had failed to take the time to learn the required vocabulary words, I remembered that one of the NON-naughty words from the song was among the test vocabulary words. I hummed a few bars of the song and, *voilà*, the word resurfaced and I aced the test.

Along the same line, as an ESL (English as a Second Language) instructor decades ago, I had a cassette of 'Hard to Learn that English as a Second Language Blues'. Each song focused on a different English challenge. My students liked the use of music.

When I taught a beginning French class once, I used some Maxime Le Forestier and Yves Duteil songs, introducing both language and culture."

A MULTIMEDIA APPROACH

From Janie Snowden, Marblehead, Massachusetts

"My language tip is seeing French movies subtitled in English...but, the trick is to change the subtitle language to French instead of English on my TV so that I can READ, as well as hear, what they're saying in French. Since I'm a visual learner, I can more easily understand what's being said if I can read it at the same time. Hearing French spoken quickly (and maybe with slang or a particular accent) can be impossible for me unless I actually see the words.

I also listen to French radio, and read as much in French as I can. Books with lots of dialogue are great so the language is something you'd actually use in a conversation that day."

SEIZING OPPORTUNITIES

From Kathy, Smyrna, Tennessee

"I studied French through junior high and high school, but I thought I had forgotten it all. However, many years later, I had a great opportunity: my employer (recently acquired by a French company) offered on-site French lessons. I took them up on it; and almost 20 years later, I'm pretty much fluent!

So what has helped the most? Certainly, the on-site classes have been great, but not everyone can afford such a luxury. I have found that attending meetings of the Alliance Française has been useful. There are chapters all over the U.S. Even though the monthly meetings do not provide enough conversation, they do provide the opportunity to network and find other people who want to meet just for conversation. Here, in Nashville, there is a group that meets every Saturday morning for coffee and 'French-speak'.

The best thing language learners can do is to forge friendly relationships with people who speak the language fluently, preferably with native speakers. Then, in social situations, we can immerse ourselves in conversation. I find that these people are pleased that we want to learn their language, and are happy to help us as we fumble along. In turn, they appreciate help with English. This process can be frustrating at first; but it has helped me be much more confident in my ability to 'go with the flow'."

LANGUAGE LEARNING FOR THE "CHRONOLOGICALLY CHALLENGED"

From Herm Meyer, of the blog Poems, Photos and Stuff (http://herms-rhyme-thyme.blogspot.com)

"Being 'chronologically challenged' (i.e., old), it's more difficult for me to learn French, but I keep whaling away at it.

My first experience with French was when I was assigned to NATO in Fontainebleau, France, for almost a year way back in the 1950's. We were not allowed to go off base in uniform so I bought French clothes and blended in with the French. I spent lots of time in Paris and with the help of my *petite amie* (girlfriend) I learned a lot of French. What a great experience that was!

Unfortunately, that was a long time ago and I didn't keep it up. A couple of years ago I decided to seriously learn French.

There is a wealth of information on the internet for learning a language. I'm at a point now where I'm finding audio books and stories very helpful. Online I listen to French short audio stories, do language exercises, and follow French blogs. An mp3 player loaded with French is also a helpful tool."

IT'S SHOWTIME!

From Anita Nagarajan, India, of the blog Funderful World (http://funderfulworld.wordpress.com)

"Read and present an article (interview or stories) about a topic that you love, in the language that you are learning.

You will be enthusiastic because it is a topic of your choice (and liking!). You will learn a lot of related vocabulary (and possibly, grammar). Your speaking skills will improve when you prepare for and actually present the topic to an audience (which could be your teacher, friends or colleagues who are familiar with the language).

For example, I love the Metro and I am learning French, so I chose a mini project on the Paris Metro. I must admit that I had a whale of a time! Of course, it helped me immensely in improving my reading and speaking skills in French."

A RECIPE FOR LEARNING

From Rachel of the blog And Then Make Soup (http://andthenmakesoup.wordpress.com)

"I'm in a weekly informal French conversation group with folks who mostly speak much better French than I do. I also find that if I want to learn new vocabulary I do best by struggling through recipes. And I can get French TV on my phone! It all helps."

DARE TO SPEAK, EVEN INCORRECTLY!

From Ellen Van Thiel, Burgundy and Virginia

"Only living in France five months a year makes it hard. My husband is Dutch, and hearing a lot of Dutch spoken in our household is very confusing as I spent 15 years living part time in Holland and trying to learn that language.

I think I learned the fastest and best and easiest with language learning CDs. I kept them in my car after I used them in the house and that way could review lessons in a very easy way and it really helped me retain the little bit I know today. Studying one-to-one with a native French speaker was the second best thing. This past summer I just jumped in and started to speak, correctly or not, and people usually understood what I was trying to say and corrected me if I asked. Strangers would correct me if I didn't ask! It was always appreciated. As with Dutch, I think exposure over time will eventually shift the balance in a positive way if I keep plugging away at it."

FIND A SUPPORT GROUP

From Sally Watling in Burgundy

"We have a weekly group who read and translate the newspapers, keep journals (mini ones) which we read out to the group, and go over grammatical points causing us problems. I also have the car radio tuned in to a French station so that when I am pottering around the lanes I am hearing French. I don't think that any one method is better than another but for me the two important factors for success are working regularly and spending as much time as possible listening to French."

A FRENCH TEACHER'S SURPRISING ADVICE

From Barbara Kelly

"About learning a language: forget the grammar. Studying the grammar is akin to studying the wiring inside your telephone. Just launch forth and say what you have to say. You can learn to conjugate the verbs later when you're back from your vacation!"

WHAT HE DID FOR LOVE…

From Clyde King, Orlando Florida

"I took French in high school in Atlanta with Thelma Kelly. We had to take and PASS two years of language. Well in the 10th grade Jim Wansley convinced me that Latin would be a push-over. I did not realize at the time how smart Jim was until the first day of Latin and I knew I was in big trouble.

So my junior year I decided French was the way to go, I believe based solely on the fact that Lois Feely (she loved me) was taking French. I somehow struggled through the first year but dreaded the second. I won't bore you with all of the details but the first three quarters were: C, D, D. I also hate to admit it but that performance was accompanied by tutoring from the student teacher. How am I doing! Anyway I really stepped it up the last quarter, understanding that even though I had been accepted to college I wasn't going anywhere until I passed French. So I really buckled down and got serious and got a C- for the last quarter and was able to graduate!!! Miss Kelly called the day before graduation to give me the news. My father applauded and mother just shook her head. It seems Mother thought that the fact that I took Miss Kelly cookies when she was in the hospital with a get-well note written in French (by Lois Feely) might have done more for my passing than my academic efforts. I had to remind my mother that she baked the cookies herself! Anyway you need to keep in mind the only thing I remember is, *Je ne comprends pas.*"

Which brings us to the end of the advice and tips from our contributors. I sure hope you fare better than my friend Clyde, above, and I hope he'll be buying this book.

In the next chapter, you'll find reviews of the many educational aids, programs, apps, and ideas to make language learning easier.

"Learning is a treasure that will follow its owner everywhere."
Chinese Proverb

Chapter 5

Your Language Learning Toolbox: A "Best of" Resource Guide

There are so many resources available in print, online, and on-site for various languages that's it's impossible to make a dent in them here. So I've focused instead on a highly subjective "best of" list, based on my personal experience and on that of my panel of experts, readers, and fellow language students.

Best Translation Dictionary:

I'm a huge fan of the **Ultralingua** dictionaries (www.ultralingua.com). There are electronic versions for your computer and smartphone that are super handy and very thorough; there is an online dictionary as well. In addition to definitions, the dictionaries include many phrases and example sentences, verb conjugations, flash cards and more. Almost all the expat learners I know use them. If you want to check out their programs, they offer a free trial.

Best Apps for Organizing Your Study or for Collecting Phrases, Words, and Questions:

You'll need a place to quickly jot down questions for a teacher, words to look up, phrases to remember, and so on. For notes like this I like **Paperdesk** (http://webspinneronline.com/paperdesk) for iPad or iPhone, which can be organized into notebooks on different topics.

To fully organize and track your studies, a good choice is **My Language Notebook** (http://my-language-notebook.software.informer.com). Or use a general organization application like **Evernote** (http://evernote.com) that will allow you to make lists and also to clip lessons from websites. It's de-signed to work across all your devices.

To make collecting words and phrases fun, my step-daughter Kelly swears by the app **Quizlet** (http://quizlet.com), which she uses with our grand-kids to help them study. You can apply Quizlet to any subject, it's a system to help with self-study. You can set up flashcards with words or phrases for example—you supply your own content.

Best All-round FREE Resources for Language Learning:

The language learning programs at **About.com** (www.about.com/education) would be super at any price, but they're free. The site has programs for many different languages. (Laura Lawless is the French expert, http://french.about.com.) These are comprehensive language learning programs, complete with regular lessons, grammar overviews, references, conjugations, and common phrases. The self-tests are useful and fun, too. One excellent feature: you can sign up for an email subscription, and get periodic lessons in your inbox. Great for catching your attention when you "forget" to study!

The **BBC** has a fabulous language learning site (www.bbc.co.uk/languages), with fun videos at every level. AND you'll learn something about the country of your target language, as the topics offered cover skills like shopping, buying a house, or dating.

There are podcasts of all sorts for language learning. Try the **Coffee Break** series at Radio Lingua Network, (http://radiolingua.com) and courses at **iTunes U** (http://www.apple.com/education/itunes-u).

Don't forget your **public library**, which may have books, software, and other audio-visual resources to check out.

Best Interactive Online Learning Programs:

Yabla online language immersion (www.yabla.com) is all about fun, and it's offered in a number of languages. It's fresh and hip, with amusing video vignettes. You can see a feed of spoken words with the videos, and you can slow down or speed up the speaker. This is a great feature if you need to work on comprehension and pronunciation.

You can join up with an online learning group at **Livemocha** (http://livemocha.com). Or learn by watching videos; you can even sign up for a private online tutor.

An online learning community is the core of **Italki** (www.italki.com), and many of the services are free. You can take Skype lessons from an overseas teacher or find an online language partner.

Best Places to Find Kindred Spirits for Conversation:

Meetup.com (www.meetup.com), which is a general meet-up site for many topics, has hundreds of language groups listed, all over the world, for any language.

There are a host of new language exchange websites aiming to hook up native speakers for language practice, both online and in person. Try **Verbling**, (www.verbling.com) which offers free practice and online classes. The **Conversation Exchange** (www.conversationexchange.com) will find you a partner for face-to-face conversation, live text chat, or voice chat. They'll find you a pen-pal if you prefer. The **Polygot Club** (http://polyglotclub.com) hosts real-life events around the world for language exchange, or will pair you with a native speaker.

Most Exciting New Way to Learn a Language:

Go MOOC hunting! "Massive Open Online Courses" are online university classes. You can choose from five languages at the Massachusetts Institute of Technology, for example; or study French at Carnegie Mellon. Some of these programs are free. This area is exploding so fast that new sites are probably popping up as you read this. Find lists of programs at sites like

Online Universities (www.onlineuniversities.com), **Coursera** (www.coursera.org), or **Open Culture** (www.openculture.com). There is also **World Wide Learn** (www.worldwidelearn.com/language-courses), **edX** (started by Harvard and MIT, www.edx.org), and **Udacity** (from Stanford, http://www.udacity.com). Not all offer language classes now but they are rapidly expanding.

Best Language Textbooks:

The **Dummies** books are favorites of mine (www.dummies.com/store). OK they may not be the most sophisticated textbooks around, but they're generally fun and upbeat to read, and laid out in a straightforward, understandable, logical way. They typically come in levels, too, and now in apps for your smartphone. I also look for good university textbooks.

The Top Eight Comprehensive Language Learning Programs to Consider Purchasing:

You're getting serious now—perhaps you want to purchase comprehensive language learning software. Here are some fine choices to consider. These programs are up to the minute, some with live and interactive choices, as well as self-study. NOTE: your public library probably has some of these language programs which you can check out for free.

Which you choose depends on your learning style, your needs, your budget, and how you will use the language. Some offer a wider range of services. Some are lighthearted and fun, some are for the serious scholar or for the business person. All offer multiple languages.

FLUENZ (www.fluenz.com)

Fluenz is a small, passionate company, offering "boutique" language learning emphasizing one-on-one instruction and an innovative approach. They go the extra mile to keep it lively and to avoid boredom.

The Fluenz philosophy: "We look at each language, be it Chinese or Italian, and take it apart from the point of view of English. We ask ourselves common sense questions: How does Italian work? What's challenging in Spanish? We then create a path through each language that makes sense to an English speaker trying to learn it. This takes a lot of time, but it's the only way it can be done."

I like that idea, and I also like this statement, which tells me you're likely to get honesty from them, instead of marketing spin: "We'll never tell anyone that something is easy when it actually takes real work to master."

BERLITZ (www.berlitz.com)

Berlitz has been around for 130 years. They invented a technique they call the Berlitz method, which is conversationally based. They have software programs, a virtual classroom program with group or individual lessons at any level, and a multitude of other services.

Choose this program if you like the tried and true, and lots of learning options. I'm a Berlitz fan myself.

PIMSLEUR (www.pimsleur.com)

Recommended by many folks who contributed to this book, Pimsleur is a program with a strong emphasis on the importance of memory. Through questions and responses, they hope to move the language from your short-term and into your long-term memory.

ROCKET LANGUAGE
(www.rocketlanguages.com)

Rocket language started out with Spanish in 2004 and they now offer 11 languages. Their approach is fun and upbeat. As their name suggests, they hope to get you up to speed quickly, so it's a good choice for those who want to learn a language with travel in mind.

TELL ME MORE (www.tellmemore.com)

Based on research, this is a serious program based on models used in the government and the military. Communication is their focus.

TRANSPARENT LANGUAGE
(www.transparent.com)

Transparent Language is a no-nonsense, research based learning program based on neuroscience, specifically the declarative memory and the procedural memory.

MANGO (www.mangolanguages)

This program, emphasizing everyday speaking skills and local culture, is often available at public libraries.

ROSETTA STONE (www.rosettastone.com)

A balanced comprehensive program offering a range of skills, using a technique they call Adaptive Recall. There is an emphasis on immersion and on associating words with images, as opposed to translating. Visual learners may like the pictorial aspect. This popular program gets high marks from many of my panel of experts and students. But it is sometimes criticized as being overly simplistic. The newest online version gives you live time with a native speaker, which is so important.

Best Language Learning Apps:

There are so many great apps! Many of our contributors are partial to foreign language **Scrabble** (https://itunes.apple.com/us/app/scrabble) for fun, and **Mindsnacks** (www.mindsnacks.com) for a unique learning experience (seven languages available).

Best Ways to Study the Culture of Your Target Country:

We have four winners in this category.

1) **Travel** there and talk to the natives!

2) **Subscribe** to magazines designed for expats, such as *France Magazine* (www.francemagazine.org) or *Living Spain* (www.livingspain.co.uk) for example. These are typically dedicated to travel, culture, and language. Of course there are plenty of books on the subject as well.

3) **Follow blogs and websites.** There are so many fabulous ones now, by expats and natives, that really take you deep into the culture and language of a country. Surf around and subscribe to the ones that speak to you. Amit Schandillia's blog called Always Spanish (www.alwaysspanish.com) is a good example. It's devoted to both language learning and to the Spanish culture.

4) **Keep up with the current events and news** in the country or countries of your target language. Read the news in English, or in your new language if you can. There are news sites online in English for most major countries. A good site for this is *The Local* (www.thelocal.com), which offers the news in English from a choice of seven countries. Or, you can use a news aggregator which can be personalized. Google News (https://news.google.com) is an example. You can set up key words so it will alert you when articles of interest come out (e.g. choose key words like "Mexico", "Japanese", "Italian politics", "German history", and so on).

Best Places to Find Bilingual Books for Casual Reading:

These clever books have English on one page, a translation on the facing page. Online book sellers will have them; search for "dual language" or "bilingual" books, in your language.

If you're visiting the country where your language is spoken, you're likely to find a good selection at the larger bookstores, since the natives will be buying them to learn that universal language that's on the facing page, English.

Best Gift You Can Give Your Kids/Grandkids:

Learn a second language together!

Best Way to Make Language Learning a Family Project:

Check out this little book: *52 Weeks of Family French* (available at www.amazon.com, there's also a **Spanish** and a **German** edition), with bite-sized lessons that families can do together.

And finally, a few just for FRENCH learners:

Most Gorgeous Location for French Immersion:

The **Institut de Français**, at Villefranche-sur-Mer between Nice and Monaco, is lovely—and challenging (www.institutdefrancais.com). You can stay two weeks but they recommend a month. Warning: those views of the Mediterranean are sure to distract you. Alumnus Beth Craig says, "The best language experience I had was three weeks at the Institut de Français in Villefranche-sur-Mer. It was INTENSE, but one of the best experiences of my life. After that I followed up with THEIR teachers for private lessons, and I will continue to do so."

Most Amusing Way to Study French when You're in Paris, Nice, Lyon, or London:

Try the clever language exchange program called **Franglish** (www.franglish.eu). Held at cafés, it's based on the speed dating model, but with language learning as the goal. You are both teacher and student. You sit down with a native French-speaking partner, speak French for seven minutes, switch to English for seven minutes, then rotate to the next table. Now how fun is that! Coming soon to more French cities, and it's also in London and Cambridge. Be sure to reserve ahead, the sessions fill up quickly.

Best French Blogs:

Oh my, there are just too many wonderful ones to mention here, though I do talk about them regularly at my own blog at **Southern Fried French** (www.southernfriedfrench.com). There is one, however, specifically targeted at language lovers: Kristin Espinasse's fun blog, called **French-Word-a-Day** (http://french-word-a-day.typepad.com). She sends out a post three times a week featuring a French word or phrase, accompanied by a heart-warming story of her life in Provence. When you visit her site, be sure to subscribe and to check out her books as well.

Two Quick, Quirky Videos to Fluff Up your French and Make You Smile:

Dansons les Capucines, A hilarious cat video dubbed by a couple of Frenchmen. You really must watch this one! You'll learn a bit of French, including some useful slang.
(www.youtube.com/watch?v=KIePsbJSS04)

L'art de la Bise, A funny cartoon primer on how to master the art of French social kissing.
(www.youtube.com/watch?v=b9m0OEpE0z8)

"Language is the road map of a culture. It tells you where its people come from and where they are going."

Rita Mae Brown

Chapter 6

If you're an Expat, or an Expat Wannabe

If you're an expat, you're lucky in language. Life will be full of learning opportunities. But English has become so universal that, depending on where you live, it may still take some effort to immerse yourself. Here are some thoughts on maximizing language learning in your host country.

If You're Going to the Countryside: Live in a village

When we first dreamed of moving to France, our friend Margaret, who had lived in France for 20 years, cautioned us: live in a village! In the French countryside, many of the houses for sale, especially the good bargains, are what the French call *isolée*, meaning they sit alone in a rural environment. It may be a lovely, private setting, but you won't encounter neighbors every day. Living in a town or a village, even a small one, there's always someone passing by. It gives you constant language practice and easy introductions to the locals. We took Margaret's advice and we've been grateful for it ever since.

Be a Joiner

My Dutch friends Gerard and Maria live in a small hamlet and have joined the local village social committee, where they are forced to interact only in French. Any volunteer organization is great for this purpose. Also the locals will be likely to accept you as one of their own if you're willing to roll your sleeves up and work for the community.

Let Go of Perfection

My friend Ali spoke slowly when she first moved to her French village, almost painfully so, trying to get everything perfect (as I did, and most expats I know). Finally her French friends said to her, "Just talk, we'll understand you!" Most of us who've advanced to conversation in our language learning can relate to that. I think most new speakers get to a point where they decide to go for a natural, conversational speed, errors be damned. It was when I reached this point that I really began to relax with the language. And don't forget that making mistakes is one of your best learning tools.

My husband is very smart, but he is not, and never will be, much of a linguist. But he cheerfully jumps in and communicates here in France, and his comprehension skills especially have gotten very good over time. Only because he is persistent and fearless has he been able to communicate, and enjoy the experience. As he often says, at his age no one is going to give him a bad grade, or judge him on this particular skill, when he excels at many others.

Find Your Balance

In your new country you may be drawn to an international expat group that speaks English, and it will feel comfortable as a result. That's fine, but try to balance it with friends who are natives, too. And invite the natives over! When we first began to tackle the "All French Evening", with only the two of us to handle a group of French speakers by ourselves, we were terrified before and exhausted afterwards. Now, such occasions are easy. Making yourself get through it in the beginning is the biggest hurdle. If you want to make it a little easier when you invite native speakers, be sure there's at least one bilingual guest in the crowd to rescue you when you get lost.

With our European expat friends, who have various native languages but all speak English, we have the rule that if there's even one French person at the table, everyone speaks French. I should note we don't always succeed in keeping the rule, but we try.

Make Contacts through a Conversation Group

If you want to meet others in your new community, finding a group language class or conversation group is one of the best ways to do it. Expat communities tend to be friendly and open, and once you become a part of the group, you'll meet expats who can introduce you to the locals.

Immerse, but Know Your Limits

Try, if you're courageous, to go for TOTAL immersion. We met a British couple once who moved to France and decided that English would be completely forbidden in their home for the first year. Books, newspapers, magazines, TV, radio, even their conversation at dinner together: all French all the time, no English was to come through the door. I personally could NOT do this and maintain any semblance of sanity, but they were determined to stick to it and it paid off for them. If it's too intense for you, try a day of total immersion once a week.

Find an Angel

Almost every expat I know managed to find a local "angel" to help them through those first difficult months—that period when you have to figure out how to get internet service, or set up utilities, or find out where the best hardware store is located. All these activities require a new, specialized vocabulary. Our angels were Nicole and Pierre, the owners of the Château de Balleure where we lived, though many other friends were helpful as well. Other expats we know have made friends with local shopkeepers, or relied on a friendly neighbor. If you can locate such a person before you move, all the better. I imagine that whatever the country or culture, you'll find people are willing to help a new resident. Just be sure to return the favor in some way!

Maximize Your Interactions

Speaking of angels, Nicole, who teaches French to me and to many expats in this area, offers some advice:

"Listening to the same person again and again is helpful because you get to know her/his way of talking, and understanding becomes easier. Be selective about who you are talking to at first. Choose the ones who express themselves simply and clearly. If you meet people with a strong accent, try to avoid them for as long as you can. And kids! They are terrible to understand!

"Try to find any opportunities to talk and do something at the same time (cooking, gardening, exploring, shopping...), whatever your interests are. You'll be more eager to learn vocabulary about something you like doing with somebody sharing a similar interest, and in addition you can actually see what you are talking about and have fun. Leave conversation about politics or philosophy for better days."

And she concludes with the advice that we all know, but it's hard to follow: "Avoid people who are speaking your native language, so that you are forced into the new one."

"The limits of my language are the limits of my world."
Ludwig Wittgenstein

Chapter 7

Daring to Move Forward with Language Learning

I hope that in reading this book, you've put together a plan to jumpstart your language learning. You've chosen the techniques that resonate with you, and gained some wisdom from the fellow students who contributed here, and taken a look at the available resources.

We've examined what learning a language can do for you: sharpen your mind, make traveling more fun, expand horizons and cultural awareness. But it can do more than that, for you and for others. Speaking a second language can make you a better citizen of the world, and a kind of ambassador for your own language and country. You will understand a new culture and people better because you can truly enter their world. You'll be able to help foreigners understand your own culture.

I hope this book has armed you with the tools you need to make learning a language easier, more enjoyable, and more efficient. It is my wish for you that you'll share your new language knowledge with fellow students, family and friends, and foreigners who cross your path. In your language journey and in all your other travels, I wish you much success.

Acknowledgements

Special thanks go to my friend and editor *extraordinaire*, Bennett Gates, and to my IT department, also known as my husband, Ron. And big hugs to my son-in-law Paul and my step-daughter Kelly, for paving the way with Kelly's own eBook adventure, Sailing to Jessica (www.sailingtojessica.com).

To all the loyal readers of my blog at Southern Fried French, especially those who contributed comments for this book and regularly add wisdom, musings, and recipes to my weekly posts: my deepest thanks for being part of the community, and this book.

Thank you to all my fellow students at "Ecole Nicole" and other dear friends who contributed comments and lent support to this project.

Joe Daggett and Dr. Michael Armstrong shared their professional advice for the book, and I was thrilled to have their input.

Kristin Espinasse of the blog French-Word-a-Day (http://french-word-a-day.typepad.com), always an inspiration, was especially helpful in originally sending my blog out into the world.

And finally to my own much-loved French teachers, Nicole and Pierre Balvay, the owners of the Château de Balleure, who with infinite patience are helping this particular used brain to acquire a second language.

About the Author

Lynn McBride has a master's in education from the University of Georgia, teaching experience, and has worked for many years as an editor for Meredith Publishing (*Better Homes and Gardens* et al). She is also a free-lance magazine writer for US and British home and travel magazines, and she blogs at Southern Fried French. She lives in southern Burgundy with her husband Ron and their cat Domino.

Made in the USA
Lexington, KY
21 February 2015